The Jungle
Upton Sinclair

Abridged and adapted by Janice Greene

Illustrated by Shelley Matheis

A PACEMAKER® CLASSIC

GLOBE FEARON
Pearson Learning Group

Supervising Editor: Stephen Feinstein
Project Editor: Karen Bernhaut
Editorial Assistant: Stacie Dozier
Art Director: Nancy Sharkey
Assistant Art Director: Armando Baéz
Production Manager: Penny Gibson
Production Editor: Nicole Cypher
Desktop Specialist: Eric Dawson
Manufacturing Supervisor: Della Smith
Marketing Manager: Marge Curson
Cover Illustration: Shelley Matheis

ISBN 0-8359-1048-2
Printed in the United States of America
16 17 18 V0CR 15 14

1-800-321-3106
www.pearsonlearning.com

Contents

Cast of Characters

Jurgis Rudkus	A young Lithuanian immigrant
Ona Lukoszaite	The fiancée and later wife of Jurgis
Elzbieta Lukoszaite	Ona's stepmother
Marija Berczynskas	Ona's cousin
Jonas	Elzbieta's brother
Antanas Rudkus	Jurgis's father
Stanislovas	Elzbieta's oldest child
Little Antanas	The son of Ona and Jurgis
Tamoszius Kuszleika	A fiddler
Jokubas Szedvilas	A friend of Jonas
The Widow Jukniene	An old woman who keeps a filthy flat
Madame Haupt	A Dutch midwife
Mike Scully	An alderman and the Democratic boss of the stockyards
Phil Connor	Ona's foreman at Brown's and one of Scully's lieutenants
Jack Duane	A safecracker who befriends Jurgis
Freddie Jones	The son of Jones, the packer
Buck Halloran	One of Scully's lieutenants
Bush Harper	Another of Scully's lieutenants
Ostrinski	A pants-finisher and socialist
Tommy Hinds	A socialist hotel owner
Mr. Lucas	A socialist speaker and former minister
Nicholas Schliemann	A socialist theoretician

1 The Wedding Dinner

It was four o'clock. The wedding ceremony was over. The people were beginning to arrive for the dinner. Cousin Marija had left the church last and gotten into a carriage. But the driver wouldn't make the horses go fast enough for her. So Marija told him what she thought of him in Lithuanian. He didn't understand. So she told him in Polish. This time he understood. They started yelling at each other. They yelled all the way down Ashland Avenue. Children heard the noise and ran after the carriage.

At last they arrived. Marija jumped off the carriage. Many people were waiting at the door. She pushed through the crowd and went inside the room.

The room was at the back of a bar. It was in that part of Chicago near the stockyards. But there is something more important we should know about this place. This is where little Ona Lukoszaite spent the happiest hours of her life.

Ona stood in the doorway. There was a light of wonder in her eyes. Her little face was pink. She wore a white cotton dress. She twisted cotton gloves in her hands. She was so young—not even sixteen. And she had just been married—to Jurgis Rudkus.

Jurgis had great, strong shoulders and huge hands. He could lift and carry a 250-pound piece of beef. But now he stood in a corner. He looked like a scared animal.

Women, young and old, came in and out of the kitchen. They carried huge dishes of potatoes, ham, rice, duck, sausages, and piles of buns. There was plenty of milk and beer. At the bar you could order all you wanted—for free.

Everyone sat down to eat. Even people who came in from the street were given food. No one goes hungry at a wedding dinner. That is the law of the old country. These poor people have given up everything else, bit by bit. But not the wedding dinner. It was the one night when life was free of cares. That night, life was only a bright bubble on a vast river. They must never give up the old ways of the wedding dinner!

People laughed and joked, children shouted, and babies screamed. Marija yelled for music. Tamoszius Kuszleika was the fiddler. He played like a crazy man. They all were immigrants, learning the ways of America. But now they listened to the music of the old country. They

3

forgot about Chicago. They thought of the rivers and the great forests of home.

It was time for the speech. Jurgis's father, Dede Antanas, got up to speak. He coughed and coughed. He was sixty years old, but he looked eighty. He held onto his chair until the fit of coughing went away. His speech was sad. He felt he would not be with his children much longer.

Soon most of the people finished eating. It was time to dance. Quickly, everyone found someone to dance with. The whole room began moving.

The older people were dressed in clothes from the old country. But not the young. They tried to wear the latest American styles. Alena Jasaityte looked pretty in a white blouse that cost half a week's pay.

Jadvyga was beautiful. She danced with her Mikolas. They had wanted to get married for a long time. But cruel accidents had almost taken the heart out of them. Mikolas was a beef boner, and that was dangerous work. It was easy for a knife to slip. Sometimes the cuts healed, sometimes not. Many times, Mikolas had been out of work because of blood poisoning.

The music stopped. Everyone took a break. Then the long dance, the *acziavimas* began. During the *acziavimas,* every man dances with the bride. After the dance, he puts money into a hat. When the night is over, there should be plenty of money for the newly married couple. The bride and groom would have a good start in their new life.

But many of the young men did not follow the old ways. They did not join the dance. They pretended they had already danced with Ona. Or they left the party.

Ona's eyes became wide with fear. She and Jurgis owed so much money for the dinner! Money for the room, for the ducks, for the music. . . .

Jurgis looked at Ona.

"Do not worry, little one," he said. "I will work harder." That is what Jurgis always said: "I will work harder!"

2 They Come to America

Jurgis had fallen in love with Ona back in Lithuania. But he had little hope of marrying her. He was a poor boy from the country, and her father was a rich man.

But then the father died. He had owed a lot of money to people. When these people had all been paid back, the family had very little money left. The family was a large one. Besides Ona, there was her brother, Jonas, and her stepmother, Elzbieta, who had six children.

The family decided to go to America. Jonas had a friend there who had become rich. Jurgis had heard of America, too. It was a place where a man could earn a lot of money in a day. And a man was free there, rich or poor. He did not have to go into the army. He did not have to hand over his money to government officials. Jurgis decided he would go to America, too. He would get married and be rich.

To earn money for the trip, Jurgis went to work on a railroad. It was awful work. The bosses were cruel and worked the men too hard. But Jurgis put up with it. When he left, he had a lot of money sewed into his coat.

That summer Jurgis, Ona, and the rest set out for America. At the last minute, Ona's cousin, Marija, came too.

They had a hard time on the trip. One man cheated them out of some money. When they arrived in New York, a policeman took them to a hotel. He made them pay a great deal to stay there.

Jonas's friend had gotten rich in the stockyards of Chicago. So that was where they went. That one English word, "Chicago," was the only word they needed to know.

A policeman showed them where to get on a train. As they came closer to Chicago, they noticed the sky growing darker. The grass outside was yellow. The land was empty. There was a strange smell: strong and raw. Suddenly the train stopped. The door was pulled open and a voice shouted: "Stockyards!"

They stepped out and noticed another strange sound. It was a sound made up of a thousand little sounds. It was the distant sound of ten thousand cattle. It was the distant sound of ten thousand hogs.

The family started up the street. Suddenly Jonas gave a shout. He ran across the street and into a shop that said, "J. SZEDVILAS,

DELICATESSEN." Elzbieta remembered that Szedvilas had been the name of Jonas's friend. Jonas came out of the shop with a fat man in an apron. At the end of the day, the two families were friends for life.

Jokubas Szedvilas said he would take them to the widow Jukniene's. It was not a nice place, he said, but it would do for now. Elzbieta said quickly that the less money they had to pay, the better. The family already knew something about America. People did make a lot of money; but everything cost a lot.

The widow Jukniene's building was awful. Usually six people slept in one room. But sometimes there were thirteen or fourteen. It was a very dirty place. People joked that the widow sent in her chickens to clean the rooms.

Later that day, Ona and Jurgis went for a walk. The street was made of dirt. Everywhere there were great holes filled with green water that stank.

There was a horrible smell from the street. Clouds of black flies filled the air. If you asked, people would tell you that this land was "made." It was made by dumping the city garbage there.

The sun went down. The ugly street was hidden in the dark. Ona and Jurgis stood looking at the lines of buildings, black against the sky. Great chimneys poured smoke like rivers into the sky. But to Ona and Jurgis, the stockyards seemed like a wonderful place—a place of power and freedom.

3   The Stockyards

Jokubas Szedvilas knew many people. He would help the family find jobs. But Jurgis felt he needed no help. The next morning he went to Brown's, one of the meat packing houses. He stood outside Brown's with the crowd of men who wanted work. One of the bosses picked him out of the crowd. He was taller than anyone else. They told him to come back the next morning. He had a job!

The three big packing houses were Brown's, Durham's, and Jones's. After Jurgis came home with his good news, Jokubas showed the family around Brown's and Durham's. He led them across the railroad tracks to a building looking out over the yards.

There was over a square mile of space in the yards. More than half of it was filled with pens full of cattle. In them were red cattle, black, white, and yellow cattle. There were old cattle and young cattle. Great bulls and babies less than an hour old.

"What will happen to all of them?" asked Elzbieta.

"By tonight, they will all be gone," said Jokubas. "They will be killed and cut up. On the other side of the packing houses are more railroad tracks. All the meat will be loaded in railroad cars and taken away.

"They don't waste anything here," Jokubas said. He told them about the hogs that were killed, too. He laughed and told a joke: "They use every part of the hog but the squeal." Everyone who showed people around the stockyards told this joke. It was the only time anyone said something funny about the stockyards.

They went inside one of the Durham buildings. Other visitors were waiting, too. Durham's was happy to let people see the packing house. It was good for business. But Jokubas said visitors saw only what the packers wanted them to see.

In a huge room, hogs were being led up a chute. At the top of the chute was a great wheel. Here, a man would grab a hog. He would chain one of its legs to the wheel. Then the wheel turned. The hog was jerked upside down. It screamed in fear. A few seconds later, another hog screamed. And another and another. It seemed the sound would break out of the room, it was so loud. This was too much for some of the visitors. The men would laugh in a nervous way. The women would stand with their hands

in fists, the tears starting in their eyes.

But the noise and the tears were nothing to the workers. They worked as fast as they could. One by one, they hooked up the hogs. One by one, they cut their throats.

Jurgis said, "*Dieve*—but I'm glad I'm not a hog!"

A line of dead hanging hogs was carried by a machine through a line of men. Each man did a single thing to the dead hog. One man scraped a leg; another cut the head off. The head fell on the floor and went through a hole. Another man made a cut down the body; another made the body cut wider; the next man pulled out the guts. These, too, slid through a hole in the floor.

When the men were finished, the hogs went into the cold rooms. These rooms were like forests of freezing hogs. First, though, the body had to be looked at by the government inspector. His job was to look at the hog's neck for signs of tuberculosis. If you asked him, this man would be glad to tell you about tuberculosis. He would tell you how dangerous it is to eat meat with tuberculosis. And while he was talking with you, you might notice that several hogs had gone by without being looked at.

The visitors went to the next floor, where the

waste parts were used. Here were the guts, fallen from the upper floor. They were used in making sausages. There was an awful smell here. The visitors went through in a hurry. Here also were left-over bits of meat. These were boiled to make soap and lard.

In another place, men cut up the hogs from the cold room. Again, parts of the hogs went through the floor to rooms below where hams, bacon and salt pork were made. Then the meat was wrapped up. It was put in boxes and barrels. At last it was loaded into railroad cars and taken away.

Next, Jokubas Szedvilas took the visitors across the street. This was where the cattle were killed. The cattle were driven into a room and shut in pens. A man with a sledge hammer would lean over a pen and hit the steer on the head. Then he moved on to the next pen. The room was filled with the "thud" of the hammer. When the steer fell, its pen was opened and it slid out to the killing beds.

The men ran from one steer to the next. First came one man to cut the throat. This was done with one quick swing. The knife moved so quickly you could not see it. There was a flash, then the bright blood ran out on the floor. The floor was half an inch deep in blood.

The other men followed. Each man made just one or two cuts. Then they ran to the next steer. In the end, each steer went to the cold rooms, like the hogs.

The visitors were taken to other buildings. In these, the animal skins were made into leather. The heads and feet were made into glue. The bones were made into fertilizer.

Jokubas told them that the great packing houses brought food to thirty million people. Jurgis listened in wonder. How proud he was to be part of such a great effort! Jurgis had a lot to learn about the stockyards.

4 A Real Home

It took Jurgis just a few minutes to learn his job. They gave him a broom. They showed him how to sweep the cattle guts into a hole. He had to work very fast, and the day was hot. But he was paid seventeen cents an hour. He came home with a dollar and a half!

At home, there was more good news. Jonas had found a job. He would start next week. Marija found a job painting cans filled with smoked beef. Only old Dede Antanas was still looking. As for Ona, Jurgis did not want her to work. It would be a sad thing, he said, if he could not work for both of them. The children should not work, either. They must go to school and learn English.

One night Jurgis came home with a piece of paper. On it was a picture of a beautiful house. The words read: "Why pay rent? Why not have your own new home?"

The house could be bought for fifteen hundred dollars—twelve dollars a month. Right now they were paying nine dollars a month for rent. The family talked and talked. It seemed that if they put all their money together, they might be able to buy the house.

The next day, Marija, Ona, and Elzbieta went to see the agent. He wasn't sure if there were any of the new houses left. If they really wanted one, they should buy very quickly, he said.

On Sunday, the whole family went to see the house. The house didn't look at all like the picture. It didn't look new, even with its fresh paint. But it did have a sink with running water. This was something Elzbieta thought she would never have.

The agent told them they must buy right away. But they were so afraid to part with their money. It took them almost a week to make up their minds. Finally, they decided to go ahead and buy.

Jokubas Szedvilas went with the women to sign the contract. While the agent watched, Jokubas read on and on. An awful thought came to him. The word "rent" kept coming up in the contract. The agent said all contracts used the word "rent."

Jokubus told Elzbieta what the word meant in Lithuanian. Elzbieta became scared. She wanted a lawyer. The agent sent for one. When the lawyer came, he called the agent by his first name. He said the contract was all right.

Elzbieta felt she was in a trap. Szedvilas asked one question after another. As far as he could tell, the contract seemed to be okay. Szedvilas asked Elzbieta if she wanted to sign. He asked her twice. She was filled with fear. They were so poor! If anything was wrong, this would be the end of them. At last, she took out the money and gave it to the agent. On the way home, she had to sit down. The fear had made her weak.

When Jurgis came home and heard the story, he went crazy with anger. He was sure the agent had tricked them. He ran all the way to Szedvilas's house. He made Szedvilas get another lawyer. The lawyer read the contract. Jurgis's body shook as he watched. At last the lawyer said something to Szedvilas.

Szedvilas said, "It's all right." Jurgis sank into a chair. There were tears in his eyes.

The lawyer said the house was called a rental until all the money had been paid. This way, it was easy to make people leave if they couldn't pay. So long as they paid, they had nothing to fear.

The house was theirs! They bought some furniture. It cost seventy-five dollars, but they could pay a little at a time. And they bought half a dozen glasses and groceries for the kitchen. It

was wonderful to fix up the house. At night, they would hang pictures and arrange chairs.

Back at the stockyards, Jurgis had never worked so hard. All the men worked very fast. They had to. If one of the men could not keep up, it was just too bad. There were hundreds waiting outside to take his place.

Jurgis did not mind the work. So he was puzzled when he heard that other men *hated* their work. And he was also puzzled when the union man talked to him. The man said the union wanted to make the bosses slow the work down. It was killing some of the men to work so fast. Jurgis said he could do the work, and so could the rest of them. The union man got angry and called him a fool.

Soon after this, Dede Antanas came home with news of a job. A man had a job for him at Durham's—but only if Antanas would give him one third of his pay. Jurgis asked his friend, Tamoszius Kuszleika, what this meant. Tamoszius said this sort of thing happened all the time. This was hard for Jurgis to believe. He tried to talk Dede Antanas out of taking the job. But the old man had been looking a long time and he wanted work—any work.

So Dede Antanas began working. After two days on the job, he came home calling Durham's every ugly name he could think of. He had learned something awful about Durham's. Dede Antanas's job was to mop the floor. All the bits of meat and trash from the dirty floor were mopped up. Then they were put in with the clean meat to be sold!

Marija, too, had a story for the family. Her friend Jadvyga told her how she had been able to get a job painting cans. There had been an Irish woman, Mary Dennis, who held the job before her. But when Mary had become too sick to work, the forelady had fired her.

Jurgis had such hopes for his new country. It was hard for him to believe these stories. But soon he saw an awful thing with his own eyes. Often cows that were about to give birth would come to the killing beds. Anyone who knows about cows knows this: meat from such a cow is not fit to eat. When one of the men noticed such a cow, he would tell the boss. The boss would start talking to the government inspector. Then the two of them would walk away. And the cow would be killed and cut up for meat, along with the rest.

People had called Jurgis a fool for believing in the packers and in America. Jurgis began to see how they might be right.

5 They Eat You Alive

About a block away from the family lived a man and his old mother, Grandmother Majauszkiene. One evening, she came for a visit. She told them one awful thing after another. First, their house was not new at all. The previous owners had been German. Next, an Irish family came. Then came Bohemians, and then Poles. Each family had tried to buy it. But in the end, they could not keep up with the money they owed.

Then she told them about the interest they must pay on the house.

"Interest!" they said. The family had never heard of such a thing. The old lady laughed.

"You are like all the rest," she said. "They trick you and eat you alive. Go look at your deed."

They got the deed. The old lady could read English. She told them they must pay interest.

The family could say nothing. They felt like they were falling into a hole. The women started to cry. It was a very sad night for the family.

It looked like Ona and Jurgis might have to put off their wedding plans. And Ona would have to find work, after all. Elzbieta thought her oldest son, Stanislovas, had better find a job, too.

Marija come home the next day with news of a job for Ona at Brown's. But, Marija warned, the forelady was the kind who liked presents. If you wanted to talk about a job, you gave her ten dollars first. The next day Ona went to see the forelady. She had a ten dollar bill, burning in her hand.

At the same time, Elzbieta had taken Stanislovas to the priest. The priest gave her a paper that said Stanislovas was sixteen—two years older than he really was. Stanislovas showed the paper to a boss at Durham's and got a job.

His only task was to put one can at a time under a lard machine. The cans filled in a few seconds. He had to stand in one spot, ten hours a day, six days a week for five cents an hour. This was his job. This was what life was like for children like Stanislovas.

All summer long, the family worked. In the fall, there was enough money for Ona and Jurgis to be married. They paid for a room. They invited all the new people they had met. The people came and went. They left Ona and Jurgis over one hundred dollars in debt. They were very much in love, but this was a sad way to begin their new life.

Winter came. For old Antanas, it was the end. The room where he worked had no heat. His cough grew worse and worse. One day, he fell down at work. He could not get up. Two men helped him get home. The family put him to bed. He kept trying to get up and go to work, but he was too weak.

At last, one morning the family woke up and saw that he had died. Jurgis spent a busy Sunday trying to find a cheap way to bury his father. Perhaps it was better that he was so busy. He had little time to feel sad.

It was a hard winter for all of them. Jurgis's job at the killing beds became more dangerous. The blood on the floor would freeze. At the same time, the air would be full of steam from the fresh blood and hot water. The men could see no more than five feet in front of them. But they still moved fast, holding their razor-sharp knives.

Another problem was the liquor stores. The men could eat dinner where they worked, in the freezing, bloody killing beds. Or they could go to a liquor store. Liquor stores were warm and friendly. They served hot food. But you had to drink. Most of the men did. Because of Ona, Jurgis kept away from liquor.

About this time, Marija and the fiddler, Tamoszius, fell in love. They were a funny pair.

He was small and not very strong. Marija was large and very strong. She could have carried him under one arm. Even her voice was huge and strong.

But when Tamoszius played his music, it was magic to Marija. Tamoszius would play for parties, taking Marija with him. Often, Marija came home with sandwiches and cake in her pockets.

One night they were coming home from a wedding and Tamoszius asked Marija to marry him. She told the family about it. She was so happy she was almost crying. They made plans to marry in the spring.

Then an awful blow fell. Marija's canning factory shut down! Marija could not believe it. But the women she worked with said this happened all the time. After Christmas, there was less work, so the factory was shut down for awhile.

At the killing beds, too, there was less work. But Brown's did not shut down. The bosses let the men stand around for hours until there was work. Of course, they were not paid for standing around in the freezing rooms.

When the union man came to Jurgis a second time, he was ready to join. Soon, every worker in the family had a union card. Jurgis never missed a union meeting. He began to learn about politics.

When Jurgis had first come to Chicago, he had voted. But he had not known what that meant. He had been working at Brown's for about three weeks. The night watchman had told him about becoming a citizen. For this, he could have a half-day off with pay.

So Jurgis went off with other Lithuanians, Poles, and Slovaks, in a great four-horse coach. They were taken to a large stone building. There, they were made to say some words they did not understand. Then they were given a fine-looking paper. It said that they were now citizens of the United States.

Later, Jurgis was taken to register to vote. Then election day came. Jurgis was taken to the back of a bar. They gave him a ballot and told him where to mark it. For this he was paid two dollars. He was very happy until Jonas told him he had voted three times—for four dollars.

Now that he was in the union, Jurgis learned what voting meant. The government was the same as in Russia. Only here, people voted for the rulers. There were two parties: the Democrats and the Republicans. The party which could buy the most votes was the winner.

In Chicago, the Democrats always won. The

top Democrat in Chicago was a little Irish man named Mike Scully. He was a very rich man. He made all the big deals around Chicago. He was the man who made the huge garbage dumps, then built houses on them. He built an ice house out of city lumber, but he never paid for it. When the newspapers got hold of that story, Scully paid a man to take the blame. Then the man left the country.

But most people in the stockyards never said a hard word about Scully out loud. A note from him could get a job at the packing houses. And the men Scully picked to work for him got the highest pay.

Scully was head of the "War Whoop League." It was the biggest club in Chicago. Before election day, hundreds of men from the club went out with lots of money in their pockets to pay for votes. It was a man from Scully's club that had paid Jurgis to vote in the last election.

People said that when the packing houses needed something, they came to Scully. At one time, the city wanted the packers to cover over Bubbly Creek. But Scully helped the packers keep Bubbly Creek for their own garbage dump. All the waste from the packing houses poured into Bubbly Creek. It was full of chemicals and dirt and grease. Every now and then the creek caught fire and burned.

Jurgis heard a lot of strange talk about the packers. People said they had secret water pipes. They stole billions of gallons of water from the city with these pipes. The newspapers had been full of stories about the pipes. But nothing had been done about it.

Every time Jurgis met a man from another part of the packing houses, he heard about a new crime.

Durham's was famous for its canned meat. But what was inside those cans was something very different than what the label said. Canned meat was made from animals which were old, crippled, or sick. Canned chicken wasn't chicken at all. It was made from such things as fat and guts of pork and beef.

Jurgis also learned about other men's jobs. Each job, it seemed, posed a different kind of danger to the worker. Men who pulled the skins off animals had swollen fingers. Men who had to carry the two-hundred-pound pieces of beef were worn out in a few years. Workers in the cold rooms came down with rheumatism.

Then there were the men who worked in the tank rooms, where lard was made. Sometimes a man would fall into one of the huge tanks. When he was pulled out, there wasn't much left of him. All but his bones ended up as Durham's Pure Lard!

By spring, Jurgis's pay had dropped from ten dollars a week to five or six. The family worried about money every day, every hour. They were never free from this worry.

The rooms of the killing beds had never been washed. The dirt and blood had been there for years. The smell was enough to knock a man over. The workers had to stay dirty and bloody all day. There was no place for them to wash their hands.

Finally Marija's canning factory started up again. But a few weeks later, she was fired. It was a long story. One day, Marija saw that she hadn't been paid for all the cans she had painted. So she went to the forelady. The forelady did nothing. So Marija went to the supervisor. No one had ever been brave enough to go to the supervisor before. The supervisor did nothing. So Marija went to him again! The supervisor got very angry. He told her to go back to work. Later that day, the forelady told Marija she was out of a job. First Marija was angry. She said she would come to work anyway. But in the end, she sat on the floor and cried.

This was a bad time for Marija to be out of work. Ona was going to have a baby soon. Jurgis wanted to have enough money for a doctor.

After many weeks, Marija found a job cutting

beef. Most of the time, this work was given to men. But one of the bosses saw how strong Marija was. He fired one of his men and put her on the job. The boss paid Marija a little more than half of what he had paid the man. Tamoszius and Marija had to put off getting married.

Ona was having a hard time at work, too. Her forelady, Miss Henderson, lived in a boarding house downtown. The boss of the loading workers, a man named Connor, lived with her. Connor was a big, red-faced man who worked for Scully. When there was little work at the factory, many of the women worked in the boarding house. These women were friends of Miss Henderson. They made things hard for good people like Ona. But Ona never told Jurgis about this. She was afraid of what he might do.

One morning Ona stayed home from work and had the baby. Jurgis got a doctor to help, just as he had wanted. The baby was a fine, healthy boy and looked just like Jurgis. They named him Antanas after Jurgis's father. Jurgis could have looked at his baby for hours. But because of work, he only saw baby Antanas on Sundays.

Ona had to go back to work after one short week. She had no time to rest after the baby. She was never strong again.

6 A Used Machine Part

It was summer. There was more work for Jurgis now. But not as much as the summer before. The packers gave jobs to more and more men. New men came every week to learn the jobs at the packing houses. Some day these men would be used to break a strike.

But Marija was making good money. She even had enough to put some in the bank. One day, she saw a huge crowd in front of her bank. People told her there was "a run on the bank." She asked, did that mean there was something wrong with the bank? They were not sure, but they thought so. Could she get her money out of the bank? Nobody could say.

Marija was sick with fear. She stood on the long line in front of the bank for a day and a half. At last she reached the window. The teller put all her silver dollars in her hands. Then she found out there had been nothing wrong at the bank at all. A policeman arrested a man in the bar next door. A crowd of people had stayed to watch and started this rumor.

Jurgis and Ona had money in the bank, too.

They had paid off their furniture. Election day had come again. Jurgis had made half a week's pay from that. By now, he knew it was wrong to sell his vote. But what difference did his vote make?

The days were getting shorter. Winter was coming. A week before Christmas, there was a great storm. The streetcars were not working. Jurgis walked through the deep snow to go to work. He carried Ona on his shoulder. She was wrapped up in blankets. Stanislovas hung onto his coat. When the storm was over, Jurgis felt he had won.

Then the family's hopes were wiped out by a cruel accident. One day in the killing beds, a steer got loose. The men jumped out of the way of its horns. Jurgis jumped too and twisted his foot. He tried to keep on working, but the pain was too much. The company doctor looked at the foot. He told Jurgis to go home and stay in bed.

Day and night Jurgis lay in bed thinking about money. How would the family get along without his pay? There was only one good thing about staying home. At least he was able to see more of his baby, Antanas.

One morning, another storm hit. Jonas, Ona, and Stanislovas went out to work. About noon,

Ona and Stanislovas came back. Stanislovas was crying with pain. His fingers had begun to freeze. He held them close to the fire. They warmed up, but the pain made him scream. After this, Stanislovas could never move his fingers as he had before. And he had an awful fear of snow. Jurgis had to beat the boy to get him to go to work.

One Saturday night, Jonas did not come home. At Durham's, they said he had picked up his pay. That was the last the family heard of him. The family felt Jonas had left to find a better life. They did not blame him. But now they had less money than ever. They were borrowing from Marija again, and this was putting off her marriage.

They took the two boys, Vilimas and Nikalojus, out of school. The boys found work selling newspapers. They would leave home about four in the morning and come home late at night. They made about twenty or thirty cents; forty cents if they were lucky.

In April, Jurgis's foot was strong at last. He went back to Brown's, but his job was gone. He asked around and stood outside with the other men. There was no job for him. Jurgis felt like the packing houses were a great machine. Now that he had been hurt, he was a used machine part. And he had been thrown away.

Jurgis asked for a job everywhere. There was only one place he hoped he would never have to work. It was the fertilizer plant at Durham's. But one day, when Jurgis came around the fertilizer plant, the boss called to him about a job.

Jurgis was told to shovel fertilizer into a cart. He set his teeth and went to work. The air was full of fertilizer dust. They gave him a sponge to tie over his mouth. But the dust filled his ears. It rained on his eyelids and mouth. He could not see the cart. He had to feel for it with his hand. In five minutes, his head began to hurt. In half an hour, he threw up from the smell. But he kept going. He had been out of work for four months.

Going home in the streetcar, people looked at him in disgust. They got up and left him alone. He smelled awful. Days went by before he could stand to eat. His head hurt all the time.

About this time, the family began to worry about Vilimas and Nikalojus. They were downtown night and day. It was a long way home. Sometimes they stayed downtown all night. They would sleep under a wagon. They were picking up the ways of the street. Jurgis felt that soon they would not be coming home at all. So Elzbieta thought she should find some work. That way, the boys could go back to school in the fall. The daughter, Kotrina, would stay at home with her little brother and Antanas.

Elzbieta got a job making sausages. Now the family learned even more about the meat that the packers sold. Elzbieta told them how the meat used for sausages lay in piles. Rats would run all over it. The workers would give the rats bread with poison in it. The dead rats would go right into the sausage.

All day long, Elzbieta stood at a sausage machine. She would go off to work in the dark morning with Ona and Jurgis. It was dark when they came home. Right away, they fell asleep. Sometimes they even fell asleep with their clothes on. The next day it would be the same thing all over again. Six days a week, year after year.

Jurgis began to drink. When he drank, he could forget how much his head hurt. It seemed as though his life belonged to him again. But then he would come home. He would see the sad eyes of his family. He would think about how much money he had spent. Then he would feel worse than ever.

He began walking with Ona, so that he could walk past the bars without going inside. Ona, too, was having a bad time. She and Jurgis had little to say to each other these days. He was always tired. She wondered if he still loved her.

That summer, Ona began to cough all the time, the way Dede Antanas had. But there was something which scared Jurgis even more. She would lose control of herself. She would have fits of wild crying. She could not stop. To Jurgis, she looked like a hunted animal. This went on for months. Elzbieta told Jurgis it was all because Ona was going to have another baby. But he did not really believe her.

One morning before Thanksgiving, there was a snow storm. Jurgis came home after having two drinks. He fell asleep. The next morning, Elbzieta shook him until he woke up. Ona had not come home that night! Jurgis ran to Brown's and waited for her. She came at last. She ran into his arms.

"What's the matter?" he said. "Where were you?"

"I couldn't get home," she said. "There was the snow. The street car stopped. I stayed with a friend—with Jadvyga." She was crying. Her body shook.

"But what's the matter?" asked Jurgis. "What has happened?"

"Oh, Jurgis, I was afraid—I was just afraid. I knew you wouldn't know where I was. I tried to get home. But I was so tired!"

It puzzled him that she was so upset. But it was nearly eight o'clock. They had already lost an hour of pay. He left her at the factory door.

A few days before Christmas, Ona did not come home again. Jurgis went to find her at Jadvyga's house. Jadvyga lived there with her mother. She could never marry Mikolas now. He had lost a hand from blood poisoning.

"Where's Ona?" Jurgis asked when Jadvyga opened the door.

"Ona?" she said. All at once, Jurgis was scared.

"She didn't come here last night, like before?"

"Before?" said Jadvyga. She looked puzzled and scared. "Ona has never come here before."

There was nothing more to say. He walked out to Ashland Avenue. The streetcars were running again. Suddenly he thought he saw Ona in a streetcar. The car was coming from downtown. The car stopped, and Ona got off. He followed her home. Ona was lying on the bed when he came into the room.

"Where have you been?" he said. Her face was white.

"I think I have been out of my mind," she said. "I walked all night."

"You have lied to me!" said Jurgis. "I saw you in the streetcar. You have been downtown! Where were you?"

She cried out. She reached her arms out and fell toward him. He let her fall on the floor. She began to cry and cry.

"Stop it!" said Jurgis. "Stop it!"

At last she stopped crying.

"You have to believe me, Jurgis. Believe that I love you! It is for the best. Please, Jurgis, please!"

He pulled her up. "Tell me where you were last night!" he said.

"I—was in a house—downtown," she said. "Miss Henderson's house. It was Connor. He took me there. He knew all about us. He knew your boss—he knew Marija's. If I didn't go with him— we would all lose our jobs.

"It wouldn't have been much longer. He was getting tired of me—the baby is coming soon— I'm getting ugly. He said that last night. And now you will kill him. You—you will kill him, and we will all die." Her face was as still as death.

Jurgis walked out of the house. Then he began to run. He ran all the way to Brown's. He ran to the loading docks. The workers stopped their work when they saw him coming.

Connor saw him and began to move. But one moment later, Jurgis knocked him down. Jurgis had his hands around Connor's neck. This was the animal who had touched his wife! Jurgis's anger made him a madman.

The other workers pulled Jurgis away from Connor. He fought them like a tiger. But at last they knocked him out. A police wagon took him to jail.

7 Jail

Jurgis was taken to a cell. At first he felt good. He could still feel Connor's neck under his fingers. But then he was filled with an awful fear. Now Ona was out of a job. And because of Connor, Marija and Elzbieta might lose their jobs, too. Jurgis could do nothing to help them.

Outside, bells began to ring. It was Christmas Eve. The bells seemed to laugh at him. Here he was, safe from the cold. They had given him food and drink. But his family was out there, cold and hungry. Why must they hurt him this way? Why couldn't they leave him outside in the cold and let his family stay in here?

The next morning, another man was put in the cell. He was young, with a light brown mustache and blue eyes.

"Well, pal," he said. "Good morning."

"Good morning," said Jurgis. The other man looked around.

"There's an awful smell in here," he said.

"It's me," said Jurgis. "I work—or used to work—in the fertilizer plant."

"I see," said the man. "So you're an honest worker!"

"What are you?" asked Jurgis.

"Me?" he laughed. "I'm a cracksman."

"What's that?" asked Jurgis.

"Safes," the man laughed again. "I break into safes."

The man's name was Jack Duane. He acted like a gentleman, but he did not mind talking to Jurgis. Duane had once invented something. Jurgis didn't understand it very well. It had something to do with telegraphing. It was worth millions of dollars. But a large company had cheated Duane out of the invention. All Duane's money had been lost in lawsuits. In the end, Duane had become a crook.

Jurgis met many other crooks. The way they talked scared him. To them, men's souls were all for sale in this city. But Jurgis's heart was far away, calling for his loved ones.

After a week, Jurgis was put on trial. The judge was Pat "Growler" Callahan. He was almost as powerful as Scully. He didn't like immigrants.

Connor walked into the courtroom. He was wrapped in bandages. Jurgis felt his anger all over again. Connor told the judge that he ordered Jurgis's wife to leave her job because she had been rude to him. After that, Jurgis tried to kill him.

Callahan turned to Jurgis. Jurgis tried to tell

him what really happened. The judge listened to most of the story.

"Oh, I see," said the judge. "Well, if Mr. Connor took advantage of your wife, why didn't she tell her supervisor? Or why didn't she just leave the job?"

Jurgis began to tell the judge about how they were poor people. How hard it was to find work. . . .

"So you thought you'd knock him down, instead," said Callahan. "Is there any truth in this story, Mr. Connor?"

"Not a bit," said Connor.

"Thirty days," said Judge Callahan. "Next case."

Jurgis said, "Thirty days! But I have a wife and a baby, sir. They have no money."

"You should have thought of that before you attacked Mr. Connor," said Judge Callahan.

Jurgis was taken to Bridewell Jail. After ten days, a visitor came. It was little Stanislovas.

"How is the family?" asked Jurgis. The news was awful. Connor knew Stanislovas's boss. The boss had told him to leave. He was selling newspapers now, with the other boys. Even Kotrina was selling newspapers. Marija had cut her hand at work. The hand was turning green. The doctor said he might have to cut it off.

Worst of all, Ona could not find work. She was not strong enough to keep up. The family could not pay the rent, and there was almost nothing to eat.

Jurgis listened. He held onto the table. He felt sick.

"When do you get out?" asked Stanislovas.

"Not for three weeks," said Jurgis. "I'll see you then."

Jurgis took fourteen cents out of his pocket. He gave it to Stanislovas, and the boy left.

8 Everything Is Lost

At last, Jurgis's time was up. He walked many miles back to Chicago, and many more back to the stockyards. He reached the streets he knew, the streets near his home. He began to run. He turned the corner, and there at last was his house.

But what was the matter with the house? It had been gray. Now it was yellow! There had been a hole in the roof. Now it was fixed. A fat boy came out the door.

"What — what are you doing here?" Jurgis said.

"I live here!" said the boy. A window opened upstairs. A woman looked out.

"Where is my family?" said Jurgis. "I left them here! This is my home!"

But the woman knew nothing. Jurgis must be wrong, she said. This was a new house. They had told her so. Jurgis walked away. He felt lost. Then he thought of Grandmother Majauszkiene.

"Yes," Grandmother Majauszkiene said, "the family was not able to pay the rent. They went back to the widow Jukniene's. One week later, the house was painted and sold again."

Their house was gone! After all their hard work! Antanas had died working for that house. Ona was no longer strong because of her work.

There had been so many traps for them. There had been the agent who lied. There had been the interest and the extra money they were made to pay on the house. Then there had been all the tricks of the packers. There had been plants shut down, and extra workers brought in, and less pay for everyone. Everything had gone against them. And now, at last, they had lost.

Jurgis sat down on the steps of a bar. He put his face in his hands and cried. But he could not give up. There was his family. He got up and walked two long miles to the widow's house.

The widow opened the door.

"Is Ona here?" Jurgis asked.

"Yes," said the woman. Just then, there was a scream. It was Ona. Jurgis ran past the woman into the kitchen. Marija was there. Her hand was in bandages. Other women were there, too. There was another scream. It came from upstairs. Jurgis ran toward the door.

"No, Jurgis," said Marija. "You must not go up! It's the baby!"

"What?" said Jurgis. "It isn't time yet! Not for two months!"

"I know," said Marija. "But it's come just the same." She pulled him back to the kitchen. The women looked at him with fear.

"Who's with her?" asked Jurgis.

Marija did not answer right away.

"Elzbieta," she said. "We had no money for a doctor. And the midwives wanted ten, even twenty-five dollars. We have nothing. We have been begging to stay alive."

Jurgis held onto the table. He felt as if he would fall over if he let go. Ona's screams went on and on. It sounded as if she were being torn apart.

Suddenly, the widow took a rag from her pocket.

"Here, Jurgis," she said. Inside it was thirty-four cents. The other women gave him all their money, too. With a dollar and a quarter, Jurgis went off to look for a midwife.

He came upon a bar. The sign above the bar said "Madame Haupt, Midwife." Jurgis ran up the stairs, three at a time.

Madame Haupt was a very fat Dutch woman in a dirty blue dress. Her teeth were black.

"What is it?" she said.

"My wife!" said Jurgis. "Come quickly!

"It is twenty-five dollars," she said.

"I—I can't pay that," said Jurgis. "But I will as

soon as I can. I can work—"

"What is your work?" she asked.

"I—I have no work right now," said Jurgis. "I've been in jail."

"How much you have?" she asked. Jurgis told her. The woman laughed.

"I would not put on my hat for a dollar and a quarter," she said. "What you got to sell?"

"Nothing," said Jurgis. "We have nothing. But I will pay you as soon as I can."

"I don't believe you," said the woman. "Give me ten dollars and pay the rest next month."

"I can't do it!" said Jurgis. "This is all I have! You must come. My wife will die!"

"I will make it five dollars for you."

"I don't have it! I would pay you but *I don't have it!*" Jurgis's voice was loud and angry. He turned and went down the stairs.

Madame Haupt shouted to him, "Wait! I will go with you!"

They walked back to the widow's house. Jurgis tried to make Madame Haupt hurry, but she was too fat to move quickly. At last he got her into the building. She went into the room where Ona was.

The widow came to Jurgis.

"You have done all you can," she said. "You must go now. You will only be in the way."

There was a bar near the widow's where Jurgis used to eat his dinner. There, the kind barkeeper gave Jurgis something to eat. He also let Jurgis spend the night in the cellar. But Jurgis could not sleep. At four in the morning, he ran back to the widow's. The house was quiet. He ran inside. The women were still waiting in the kitchen.

"Not yet," Marija said. But a few minutes later, Madame Haupt came into the room. Her hands and arms were bloody.

"I have done all I can," she said. Nobody said a word.

"It's not my fault," said Madame Haupt. "It was too late already when I came."

"How is Ona?" said Jurgis.

The woman was angry.

"She will die, of course," she said. "The baby is dead now."

Jurgis ran into the room. Elzbieta was in one corner, crying. Ona lay on the bed, still and white.

"Ona! Ona!" said Jurgis. She did not move.

Jurgis said, "Look at me! It's Jurgis, come back—don't you hear me?" Her eyes opened. For a second, she saw him—she knew him. Then she was gone.

All night he lay beside her. He would look at her white face, then hide his eyes. He could not stand it. She was only eighteen. Her life had just begun, and now she was dead.

That morning, Kotrina came in. She had been selling papers with the boys.

"What happened?" she said.

"Have you any money?" said Jurgis.

"Yes, Jurgis," she said. "Almost three dollars."

"Give it to me," said Jurgis. The way he looked scared her. She gave him the money.

Three doors away was a bar. Jurgis went in.

"Whiskey," he said. "How much is the bottle? I want to get drunk."

But a big man cannot stay drunk for long on three dollars. Jurgis went back to the widow's house. He sat beside Ona's body. The life that he and Ona lived had changed him; he had become hard. But it had not changed her; she had kept the same hungry heart. She had always held her arms out to him for love. Every angry word he had said to her came back—and cut him like a knife.

Late that night, Elzbieta came to him. She was afraid he would leave, like Jonas had. She begged him not to leave them and his little son.

Jurgis said he would stay. He would look for work tomorrow. He would do his best for Antanas and the rest.

9 Leaving Home

The next morning, Jurgis went back to the fertilizer plant. The boss said there was no job for him. Not now, not ever.

"What is the matter?" asked Jurgis. "Didn't I do my work?" But the man would tell him nothing more.

After a week of looking, he found a job at Jones's packing house. But when he came to work the next day, the boss said, "I'm sorry. I made a mistake. I can't use you."

Jurgis was blacklisted. The men in the bars told him all about it. Knock down a boss and you're finished, they said. Now his name was on a list in every office in the packing houses. He could never work for the packers again.

Jurgis looked for work downtown. In the end, he got help from a friend. This man worked for the Harvester Trust. He talked to his boss about Jurgis, and the boss gave Jurgis a job.

Harvester Trust was a company that reformers pointed to with pride. It had a restaurant where the workers ate good food at low prices. It had a place for women workers to rest. It wasn't dirty like the packing houses.

Five thousand people worked at Harvester Trust. It made over three thousand farm machines a year. All the parts of the machines were made in different places. Where Jurgis worked, metal seats for farmers to sit on were made. His job was to load them onto a cart and push them to another room. This was child's play to him. After working at the packing houses, Harvester Trust was like heaven.

Jurgis began to hope again and make plans. He started going to school at night. He studied English and began to learn how to read. Then, nine days after his job began, Harvester Trust closed down!

Jurgis felt like giving up. What good were kind bosses when they could not keep a job for him? What good did it do to work hard? All the men's hard work had made more harvesting machines than the country wanted to buy.

Jurgis stayed in his room, feeling bad. But soon his money was going again. Little Antanas was hungry. Madame Haupt wanted to be paid.

Jurgis stayed downtown. He walked the streets of the city. Everywhere, he begged for work, any work. One day, he came home and found he had a chance for a job.

It was quite a story. A kind lady, a settlement

worker, had met the family. She had seen one of Elzbieta's children looking for food in Scully's garbage dump. The boy had told her where he lived. The lady came to visit the next day. She was a fine lady, and beautiful. She wore a hat with a bird on it. There was a long fur snake around her neck. The lady asked Elzbieta about the family. Elzbieta told her all that had happened to them. She felt bad that her story was such a sad one. But the kind woman wanted to hear everything.

In the end, the lady brought a basket of food and a letter for Jurgis. The letter was from the superintendent of one of the steel mills.

"He will get Jurgis something to do," the lady said with a smile full of tears. "If he doesn't, he will never marry me."

So Jurgis went to the steel mill with his letter. One of the men said he would see if there was a job for Jurgis. He took Jurgis through the mill.

It was a huge place, like a city. In one area, roaring kettles poured out melted steel. It looked like a great river of fire. In another area, bars of steel were cut up like bits of cheese. All around and above, huge machine-arms were flying and large hammers were crashing. Moving cranes grabbed pieces of iron with great big hands.

At last the man brought Jurgis to a place

where steel rails were made. There, one of the bosses said he could use an extra man. Jurgis took off his coat and went to work.

At first, Jurgis felt he would never adjust to working at the steel mill. The noise and heat were awful. He was scared to handle the red-hot steel. But then he got used to it. Soon, like the other men, he began to take chances.

Four days after he began the job, there was an accident. Jurgis worked near some brick ovens full of white-hot melted steel. One of these ovens blew out. Liquid fire flew through the air. Two men were hit. They screamed and rolled on the ground. Jurgis ran to help them, burning his hand.

Jurgis had to stay at home for eight days. He spent his time sleeping and playing with little Antanas. The boy was a year and a half old by now. He was loud and tough. Nothing could hurt him. He was very hard to control. But Jurgis was glad the little boy was so tough. Antanas would need to fight to get through this life.

Soon Jurgis went back to work. Winter was over now. The rains had begun, and the street was like a river. Sometimes the water was up to Jurgis's waist. But he did not mind this much. Marija had gotten a job cutting meat again. Things were looking up.

And then one Saturday night he came home to see a crowd of people at his door. He ran up the steps. Everyone was looking at him. The kitchen was full of women. All at once, he thought of the day Ona died.

"What's the matter?" he said. He heard crying. It was Marija. He started to go upstairs. The widow grabbed his arm.

"Don't go up there!" she said.

"What is it?" he yelled.

The old woman's voice shook. "It's Antanas. He's dead. He drowned out in the street!"

Jurgis went into the room and looked at the little body of Antanas. Then he walked out of the house. He walked and walked. He saw nothing.

He came to a railroad crossing. A wild feeling took hold of him. When the train stopped, he swung up onto one of the cars. The train started moving again. Jurgis began a fight with his soul. He would not cry. He would not think of Antanas or his family. He was free now. He would fight for himself. He would fight against the world that had hurt him so much.

The train went on and on. Jurgis began to smell the sweet air of the country. When morning came, the train stopped, and Jurgis got off.

At a farmhouse, a woman sold him two

sandwiches, a piece of pie, and two apples for ten cents. He walked off to a stream, where he ate his lunch and fell asleep.

When he woke up, the sun was hot in his face. All at once, he had a wonderful idea. He would have a bath! He had not had a real bath since he left Lithuania. In Chicago, there had been only the sink to wash in. He swam and scrubbed himself clean with sand. Then he washed all his clothes.

Around dinner time, he tried another farmhouse. But the farmer said, "We don't feed tramps here! Get out!" Jurgis walked off.

Behind the barn, the farmer had planted some small peach trees. Jurgis pulled every tree—over a hundred of them—out of the ground. From now on, Jurgis was going to fight. Any man who hit him would get as good as he gave.

Before long, Jurgis came to another farmhouse. This time, a farmer let him pay for dinner and for a place to sleep in the barn. After dinner, the farmer asked Jurgis if he wanted a job.

Jurgis asked, "Just for the summer? Or in the winter, too?"

"N—no," said the farmer. "I couldn't keep you after November."

"I see," said Jurgis. "When you get through

working your horses this fall, will you turn them out in the snow?"

"It ain't the same thing," said the farmer. He gave Jurgis a big breakfast the next morning for only fifteen cents. Then Jurgis said goodbye and went on his way.

This was the beginning of Jurgis's life as a tramp. He walked everywhere. He slept outside. He ate berries and stole from farms. He worked a little when he had to.

Everywhere he went, there were men who lived as he did. They told him when to steal from farms, when to beg, and when to do both. Like Jurgis, most of these men had once been workers. And, like Jurgis, they had lost everything.

Harvest time came. All the men and women in the area joined in the work. Jurgis worked eighteen hours a day for two weeks. When it was over, he made more money than he had ever made before.

One Saturday night, he and some friends went to a bar in town. There he spent a long night. His money went for drink. In the morning, not one cent was left. He felt sick and ashamed of himself.

Jurgis could not get away from thoughts of his family. One night he was caught in a rainstorm. A

Russian man let him stay in his house. After dinner, the man's wife gave their baby a bath. The little boy played in the water, talking in his baby voice. Every word went through Jurgis like a knife. All at once he began to cry. He got up and ran out into the rain. He hid in the woods and cried as if his heart would break. It hurt so much to think of his old life!

10 Hard Times

In the fall Jurgis went back to Chicago. It was getting too cold to sleep outside or in barns. After almost a month of walking around the city, he found a job.

Jurgis was told to dig tunnels for telephones. But the tunnels looked too big for telephone wires. They were eight feet high and almost as wide. And they were laid with train tracks!

A year later, Jurgis learned that the big company bosses were having the tunnels built for freight subways. They could then have their goods delivered by subway, rather than by trucks. The union that gave these bosses the most trouble was the teamsters, or the truck drivers. When the tunnels were finished, the truck drivers would no longer be needed. The factories and stores would be joined by railroad depots. The bosses would have the teamsters by the neck.

Jurgis's tunnel was a new one. That made him happy. He knew he would have a job all winter. But the work was dangerous. Usually, one man died each day from falling rocks, explosions, or run-away railroad cars. One night Jurgis was walking out of the tunnel. All at once, a railroad car from another part of the tunnel ran by. It hit Jurgis on the shoulder and threw him against the wall.

Jurgis spent Christmas in the hospital with a broken arm. It was the best Christmas he had spent in America. There was only one thing he did not like about the hospital: he was fed canned meat. Anyone who had worked in the stockyards would not give canned meat to a dog.

At the end of two weeks, Jurgis left the hospital. But his arm was in a bandage. He was out of work. He had two dollars and sixty-five cents in his pocket. He had no overcoat.

It was January 1904. The country was coming into hard times. Factories were shutting down every day. Thousands of men and women were out of work. There were few free places to sleep. People fought over them. A night on the street could mean death from the cold.

In a few days Jurgis's money was gone. He had to beg for his life. One night he was working the theater crowd. He came up to a man in a silk hat.

"Please, sir," he said. "I'm out of work and don't have a cent. . . ."

The man said in a thick voice, "Whuzz that you say?" Jurgis began his story again. The man

63

fell against Jurgis. He was young, about eighteen. He put a hand on Jurgis's shoulder.

"I'm up against the world myself, old chap," the man said. "It's a hard old world."

The young man's name was Freddie Jones. He told Jurgis that his father was away in Europe, someone named Bubby was on a honeymoon, and Aunt Polly was in the hospital having twins. Worst of all, Kitty had sent him away. He was all alone. He thought Jurgis better come home with him and have some dinner.

From somewhere, he pulled out a big roll of bills. It was more money than Jurgis had seen in his entire life. Jurgis shook with excitement. He could grab those bills and be out of sight in a minute. Should he do it? He waited a second too long.

Freddie got one bill loose. He gave it to Jurgis. It was a hundred dollar bill.

"You take it. Pay the cabbie and—hic—keep the change," Freddie said.

A cab was driving by. Jurgis shouted, and it stopped. Freddie gave an address on Lake Shore Drive and fell asleep. About a half hour later the cab stopped. Jurgis thought Freddie must have made a mistake. The house looked like a hotel or city hall. Jurgis could not believe one family lived there.

A butler in blue opened the door. He took one look at Jurgis and began to lead him outside.

"Hamilton!" said Freddie. "My friend will stay with me."

"But, Master!" the butler said.

"See that the cabbie is paid, Hamilton," Freddie answered. He took Jurgis's arm. Jurgis followed. His heart beat wildly. He had no idea what sort of place he was in.

They went into a great room. It was so bright Jurgis could hardly see at first. The walls were one huge painting. There were dogs and horses and flowers. Young women were bathing in a forest pool. Everything was life-sized. Jurgis thought he must be in a magic castle.

In the center of the room was a table, black and gold and silver.

"This is the dining room. How do you like it, hey, old sport?" Freddie said. Jurgis liked it.

"Go home and tell the people about it." Freddie said. "Old man Jones's place. Jones the packer. Beef-trust man. Ever hear of Jones the packer, hey, old chap?" Jurgis almost jumped.

"Whuzz a matter?" Freddie asked. "You heard of him?"

"I have worked for him in the yards," Jurgis said.

"What!" cried Freddie. "You! Ho, ho! Why,

that's good! Shake hands on it, old man! Governor should be here. Glad to see you. Great friends with the man, the governor. Funny things happen in this old world, don't they, old chap?" Freddie turned to the butler.

"Hamilton," he said. "Let's have some dinner. We'll have some cold meat and something to drink. Hear me, sir?"

"Yes, sir," said the butler. "But your father left orders. . . ."

Master Freddie stood up tall. "My father's orders were left to me—hic—and not to you," he said. Holding onto Jurgis's neck, Freddie led Jurgis upstairs to his study. In the center was a table covered with books. College flags were on the walls. There were sofas and chairs. Bear and tiger skins covered the floor. Beyond the room was a bedroom. And beyond that was a swimming pool.

The butler came in behind them. He watched Jurgis every second. Three other men came in. They put trays of food on the table. There was cold meat, cut thin. There were tiny bread and butter sandwiches. There was a bowl of peaches and cream. There were little cakes, pink and green and yellow and white. And there were six ice-cold bottles of wine.

Freddie sent the men away. But Jurgis saw the

butler leave the key out of the lock, so he could look through the hole.

"Now," said Freddie. "Go for it."

Jurgis looked at him.

"Eat!" said Freddie.

"Don't you want anything?" said Jurgis.

"Not hungry," said Freddie. "Just thirsty. Had some candy at Kitty's. You go on."

So Jurgis began. He used his knife and fork like two shovels. Once he got started, he could not stop. He ate like a wolf. He did not stop until every plate was clear. Freddie watched him in wonder.

"Gee whiz!" he said. He leaned back in his chair. He smiled at Jurgis and began to talk again. He told him all about his family. He went on and on until he was tired out. Then he smiled a sweet smile at Jurgis and closed his eyes. Jurgis sat still for some minutes. Then the door opened and the butler came in.

"Get out of here!" whispered the butler. Jurgis looked at Freddie. "If you wake him," the butler continued, "I'll crush your face before you're out of here!"

They walked down the steps to the front door.

"Hold up your hands," said the butler. Jurgis saw that the butler was going to search him.

He cried, "No! I haven't touched a thing in that

house. I'll not have you touch me!"

Afraid that his young master would wake up, the butler opened the door quietly. As Jurgis walked through, the butler gave him a hard kick. Jurgis flew down the steps and into the snow.

Even though he had been kicked, Jurgis was happy. He still had the hundred dollars! But then he saw what a problem that was. He had no other money and no place to sleep. How could a bum like him get change for a hundred dollars?

He walked into a saloon. "Can you change a hundred dollars?" he asked. The bartender gave Jurgis a hard look.

"Where did you get it?" he asked.

"Never mind," said Jurgis. "I've got it and I want it changed."

At last the bartender said he would change it. Jurgis asked for a glass of beer. He gave the bartender the hundred dollar bill. But the bartender gave him back ninety cents

"I want my change!" Jurgis demanded. "The rest of my hundred!"

"Go on," said the bartender. "You're crazy!"

Jurgis looked at him with wild eyes. He took his glass and threw it at the bartender's head. He climbed over the bar. The bartender hit him in the face.

"Help! Help!" cried the bartender. In a minute,

two other men came running in to join the fight, and then a policeman entered. A blow from the policeman's stick ended the fight.

The next morning, Jurgis was in court. The judge did not believe his story about the hundred dollar bill. He was given ten days in prison.

On the second day, they let him go outside to the yard. There he saw—Jack Duane! The young man was so happy to see Jurgis, he almost hugged him.

Jurgis told Duane what had happend to him.

"Hard luck, old man!" Jack said. "But maybe you've learned something."

"Yes, I've learned some things since I saw you last," said Jurgis.

The last time Jurgis was in prison, he had only thought of his family. But this time he listened to the men in prison. He was one of them now, and he would stay alive in the same way.

When he got out of prison, he looked up Jack Duane. Duane had been waiting for him. Duane was out of money, but he had a plan to get some. A man called "Papa" Hanson would hide them, as long as he was paid.

That night Duane and Jurgis went out and hid by the street. A working man came along. They let him go by. They waited in the cold until another man came along. First, they let him pass. Then they rose up after him. Duane hit the man in the head. Jurgis held his hand over the man's mouth. The man fell into his arms. Quickly, Duane went through the man's pockets. He took over a hundred dollars and a gold watch.

The next day, Jurgis and Duane read about the robbery in the paper. The man had been hit too hard. He had a concussion. He was almost frozen before he was found. He would lose three fingers from his right hand.

Because this was his first time, Jurgis felt bad about the man. Duane laughed. He told Jurgis it was the name of the game. Soon it would be like knocking out a steer.

"Still," said Jurgis. "That man never hurt us."

"He was doing it to someone else, though," Duane said. "You can be sure of that."

Duane knew some of the biggest crooks in the city. Soon Jurgis began to learn where the real power in Chicago lay. It was not with the people. It lay with those who could buy the votes and buy the leaders.

Jurgis met "Buck" Halloran. He was in politics, on the "inside." Halloran gave Jurgis a job. His job was to get pay envelopes for several different men. Jurgis would go up to the paymaster and give a name. Then he would come back later and give a different name. All Jurgis had to do was hand the envelopes over to Halloran and keep quiet. Jurgis was very good at keeping quiet.

He soon learned what a good friend Halloran could be. One night Jurgis went to a dance. He started a fight over a woman and ended up in the hands of the police. He sent for Halloran, who got him released early that morning.

One night while trying to open a safe, Duane was caught. The policeman knew him and let him get away. But the city was sick of robbers and the policemen they bought off. The newspapers set up a cry, and Duane left town in a hurry.

11 Scab!

About this time, Jurgis met "Bush" Harper. Harper was Mike Scully's right-hand man. Harper had been the night watchman at Brown's, but he was also a spy for the packers. He told them everything his union was doing.

Harper told Jurgis what was happening with the election. Mike Scully, the Democratic boss of the stockyards, had a deal going with the Republicans. The plan was to nominate a rich Democrat in the race for alderman. Scully would give this man's money to the Republicans. In return, the Republicans had to nominate a friend of Scully's, a Mr. "Scotty" Doyle. And next year, the Republicans could not nominate anyone at all, since Scully himself was up for re-election.

Harper said that what Scully really needed was someone to get the Republicans together. Someone who knew the stockyards and could work there. Someone like Jurgis. Was Jurgis interested in the job?

"But I'm blacklisted," said Jurgis.

That was no problem. The next day Jurgis went to the stockyards and met Mike Scully himself. He was a dried-up little man, with eyes like a rat. Jurgis did not know Scully was a puppet of the packers. To Jurgis, Scully was the "biggest" man he'd ever met.

Scully got Jurgis a job at Durham's. Right away, Jurgis looked up his old friends. He talked about what a good man Scotty Doyle was. And why should they vote for a rich outsider?

Jurgis worked hard, right through the election. He bought votes and voted six times himself. In the end, Scotty Doyle was elected. And how happy the workers were. They had elected a real "man of the people."

After the election, Jurgis had almost three hundred dollars in the bank. He wore a greasy red tie now. He spent his money on drink, cards, and pool. But Scully told Jurgis to keep his job at Durham's. Something might "turn up," he said.

That something was a strike. The union wanted 22 cents an hour for unskilled men, but the packers said no. After all, there were a hundred thousand men in Chicago who were out of work. They would be willing to work for less money. But the union workers went on strike anyway.

Jurgis went to see Scully. Was there a job he could do during the strike?

"See here," said Scully. "Why don't you stick

by the job you have?" Jurgis was puzzled. In the paper that day, Scully had said awful things about the packers. Now, it seemed he wanted Jurgis to continue to work for them.

"You mean work as a scab?" Jurgis asked.

"Why not," said Scully. "What's it to you?"

So Jurgis went back to Durham's. He was put in charge of the killing beds. He was a boss!

It was a strange group of workers under Jurgis. There were black men from the South. There were immigrants who did not speak a word of English. There were white-faced office workers who looked like they might pass out from the heat and the smell of blood. The packers had brought these scabs in to take the places of the workers on strike. No one but Jurgis knew a thing about killing steers.

Every day the packers brought in more scabs. They had them sleep in the buildings. They laid out cots in every inch and corner. Every night there was drinking, shouting, and fighting. And every day there were thousands of steers dying in rivers of hot blood.

Jurgis made a lot of money, but he hated himself for being a scab. He drank. He was in an awful mood. He drove his workers until they almost dropped.

One day Jurgis was told to stop his work.

Some steers had gotten loose and were in the street. The supervisor led Jurgis and his men to two waiting trucks. There were police wagons, too. Everyone drove off down the street until they came upon a large crowd. When people in the crowd saw the police, they started to run in every direction. On the ground was a dead steer. The strikers had already caught and killed the animal.

Of course the strikers could not get away with this. The police started cracking every head they saw. Jurgis jumped in and joined the fight. He and two policemen chased some men into a bar. There, they beat up a man and a woman. Then they helped themselves to some bottles and money from the cash drawer.

Later that night, Jurgis went gambling. He lost money and drank a lot. It was early in the morning when he got back to the stockyards. He was stepping into a dark room when suddenly a door opened. A man with a lantern stepped in. It was Connor!

Jurgis looked at the man who had ruined his wife and had sent him to prison. His heart jumped. He threw himself at Connor and took him by the neck. People came running in. They tried to pull Jurgis off Connor. Then a policeman

came in and hit Jurgis with his stick until he passed out.

When Jurgis woke up, he sent for "Bush" Harper. But when Harper heard that Jurgis had been fighting with Connor he said, "Connor! Not Phil Connor!"

"That's the man," said Jurgis. "Why?"

"You're in for it now, old man," Harper replied. "*I* can't help you. Connor's one of Scully's biggest men!"

Harper said that he could get Jurgis off. But Jurgis had to give him a lot of money and clear out of Durham's as quickly as he could.

Poor Jurgis was near the end of his rope now. He had no one to give him a job. There were twenty thousand men and women in Chicago who were out of work. And it was the dead of winter. He spent his money little by little on food. He grew weak. He was afraid he would starve.

When he was down to his last quarter, a man at a warehouse gave him a job. But Jurgis was too weak to work! He almost broke down and cried like a baby. He begged—for his very life.

One night he came up to a woman in fine clothes.

"Please ma'am. . ." he began.

"Jurgis Rudkus!" said the woman. It was Alena

Jasaityte, who had been at his wedding.

She said, "I give you my word, Jurgis. I would help you if I could. But I have come out without my purse. I can do something better, though. I can tell you where Marija is."

She gave him an address on Clark Street. When he knocked on the door, a young woman opened the door and let him come inside.

"Does Marija Berczynskas live here?" asked Jurgis. The woman told him there was no one there by that name. Jurgis's heart went down to his boots.

"I was told this is where she lived!" he said. There was a knock at the door. The young woman went to open it. Suddenly, she ran past him.

"Police! Police!" she screamed.

Jurgis took one look at the men in blue. He ran after her. He ran into the hall. It was full of men and women, running. Jurgis looked in one of the rooms. There was a table knocked over. Cards were all over the floor. Bottles of wine spilled on the rug.

A large woman with painted cheeks said, "To the back! Quick!" Jurgis followed her. But the police were there already.

One of them called, "You may as well quit, you people. We mean business, this time."

The police started bringing the men and women down the hall. The women were laughing and joking. But one voice rose above them all. It was a woman in a bright red dress. Jurgis recognized her.

"Marija!" he exclaimed.

"Jurgis!" she said.

For a second they stood, looking at each other.

"How did you come here?" she asked. Jurgis told her.

"Move along now," a policeman said.

Marija took Jurgis into another room. By now he had guessed what kind of a place Marija was living in. He had seen a lot of the world by now.

But they had always been good people at home, he thought. It hurt him that she should do this. Then he laughed at himself for being a fool. Who was he to be saying who was good and who was not?

"Why did you come here?" he asked.

"I had to live," she answered, "and I could not see the children starve."

"How are they? Are they all right?" Jurgis asked.

"They're all right now. I take care of them most of the time," Marija explained. "I have plenty of money now."

"Does Elzbieta know — how you live?"

"Elzbieta knows. I couldn't lie to her. It's nothing to be ashamed of. We can't help it."

Jurgis thought of the little violin player who had wanted to marry Marija.

"And Tamoszius?" he asked.

Marija said, "How would I know? I haven't seen him for over a year. He got blood poisoning and lost a finger. He couldn't play the violin anymore. And then he went away."

Jurgis said, "Maybe you thought I did you a dirty trick, running away. . . ."

"No, we don't blame you," Marija said. "You did your best. You just didn't know anything. That was the trouble with all of us. If I'd known then what I know now. . . ."

"You still would have come here?" Jurgis asked.

"Yes," she said. "When people are starving, and they have something to sell, they should sell it. Ona could have taken care of us all from the beginning."

"I—yes, I guess so," said Jurgis. He did not tell her about knocking Connor down again.

A policeman knocked on the door. It was time to go to the police station.

12 Comrade

The women were let off the next day after paying a fine. Jurgis was set free, too. Marija told him where he could find Elzbieta. But he wasn't sure he should go to her right away. Would Elzbieta think he was trying to live off her?

Jurgis thought he might spend one last night on his own. Then he would try once more for a job.

There was a free meeting going on in a hall. He went inside to rest and think about what to do. People filled the hall. When a man came to speak, they stood up, shouting and yelling. Jurgis thought they looked like fools. What did they think they were going to get out of the next election? Jurgis knew politics from the inside now.

Jurgis sat down, thought about Marija and Elzbieta, and fell asleep. Then he woke with a start. He had been snoring.

A woman with a sweet voice said, "If you would try and listen, comrade, perhaps you would be interested."

Comrade, she had called him. Jurgis peeked at

the beautiful young woman next to him. Then he looked up at the speaker on stage. He was a very thin man, with deep black eyes. His voice was full of feeling.

He said, "Comrades! Comrades! Look about you! Look at this world you are living in. Tonight in Chicago there are ten thousand men—homeless. They want to work. They beg for the chance. They are starving. They must face the awful winter cold. Tonight in Chicago there are a hundred thousand children working their lives away to earn their bread! There are a hundred thousand mothers living in misery. How terribly hard they work to feed their little ones! There are a million people who work every hour they can stand. They are wage-slaves. They make just enough to keep themselves alive. And they must live this way, cold and hungry and tired, until they die!

"Then there are the few who are the masters of the slaves. They do nothing to earn what they get. They live in palaces. They spend hundreds of dollars for a pair of shoes. They spend millions for horses and cars and boats.

"Is there anyone here who thinks this can go on forever? Do you think the masters will ever set you free? No! It is up to you! You will rise up. You will snap the ropes that hold you! You will be free!"

The speaker's words crashed like thunder in Jurgis's heart. People in the hall rose to their feet with a roar. Jurgis rose up with them. He shouted as hard as he could. He shouted and shouted until at last he could only whisper.

Jurgis had been beaten and broken. He had stopped hoping. And now all his old hopes and dreams and anger came back to him. A new man had been born.

When the meeting was over, Jurgis went behind the stage. Sitting on a chair, with his eyes closed, was the speaker.

Jurgis said, "I wanted to thank you, sir!"

A big man with glasses said, "The comrade is too tired to talk—"

"Wait," said the speaker. "You want to know more about Socialism?" Yes, Jurgis did. The speaker had him meet Comrade Ostrinski. Ostrinski invited Jurgis to his home. Ostrinski and his wife worked as "pants finishers."

Ostrinski said pants finishing was easy to learn. Anybody could do the job. So the pay was getting less and less all the time. Like all workers, Ostrinski said, he had only his work to sell. And if someone sold his work for less than Ostrinski, then the buyer would pay Ostrinski less, too. This was competition. Because of competition, the working people, the proletariats, would always be poor.

On the top were the rich and powerful, the capitalist class. They would be on top until the workers became "class conscious" and stood up together. Then they would win elections and control the government. They would put an end to private property. This would take a long time, Ostrinski said, but more people were turning to Socialism every day. There were Socialists all over the world.

Jurgis listened to Ostrinski until late that night. He saw his life at the stockyards in a new way now. He thought about his first trip to the stockyards. He had felt sorry for the hogs, which lived only to be killed for meat. Now he saw he had been like those hogs. The packers had wanted him only for his work. To the packers, a worker and a hog were the same!

The next day, Jurgis went to see Elzbieta. He was not shy about seeing her now. He wanted to tell her all about Socialism.

At first she thought he was out of his mind. Then she decided he was not really crazy, except when it came to politics. But when she saw that Jurgis planned to find work and help the family, she began to think Socialism might be a good thing after all. Elzbieta was a very practical woman.

Jurgis looked everywhere for work. At last, after a week, he had some strange luck. He was passing a small hotel when he decided to ask the owner for a job. It turned out there was a job as a porter. Jurgis was hired.

Later that day, he told Ostrinski about his good luck. When he told Ostrinski where the hotel was, Ostrinski said, "Then you've got the best boss in Chicago! Tommy Hinds!"

Tommy Hinds was a well-known Socialist leader. Jurgis became known as "Comrade Jurgis" at the hotel. His boss, Comrade Hinds, was a little man with wide shoulders, a bright face, and a very good heart.

Hinds had been fighting the rich and powerful on his own for thirty years. Then he had found Socialism. He could talk about Socialism all day and all night.

Every worker in Hinds's hotel was a Socialist. When Hinds was not there to talk about Socialism, the clerk would do it. And if the clerk was away, the assistant clerk would do it.

About that time, many cattlemen stopped at Hinds's hotel. The packers were getting a lot of money out of them these days. When they came to Chicago, they needed a cheap place to stay. Tommy Hinds would have Jurgis tell them about the stockyards and what was done to the steer meat. And while Hinds listened, he would slap his leg and say, "Do you think a man could make such things up?"

Next, Tommy Hinds would tell the cattlemen about the Beef Trust, the group of meat companies that got together to control prices. And there was also the Railroad Trust. These giant trusts were great enemies. They fought each other for control of the whole country.

Such was Jurgis's new life. He learned more and more about Socialism and was devoted to Hinds. He worked hard to keep the hotel clean and sparkling.

It would be nice to say that Jurgis stopped drinking right away. But he was just a man, not an angel. He would fight with himself not to drink.

Jurgis wanted to tell everyone he met about Socialism. But some people would just not see the light. They could not believe they were slaves, no matter how Jurgis argued. He was a hard man to be around these days.

He found out about the Socialist newspaper, the *Appeal to Reason*. He felt he must take some of these papers to the stockyards. There would be an election in a few days. The Socialists had a man running for office. Jurgis wanted to undo the work he had done last year, when he had helped Mike Scully's man get elected.

The workers had lost the strike. They were ready to hear what the paper Jurgis brought them had to say.

Jurgis went back to see Marija. He told her he had a job. Now she could leave and start a new life. But Marija shook her head. Other women had tried to leave, but someone always found out about them.

"I'll stay here until I die, I guess," Marija said. Jurgis went away with a sad heart.

At home, Jurgis was not very happy either. Elzbieta was often sick. Her boys were wild. They did what they liked. They had been out on the streets too long. But Jurgis stuck by the family. When things went wrong, he would dive into his work for the Socialist movement and feel better.

His new life was full of wonders. He would never forget the night before the election. That night he went to Mr. Fisher's house. Mr. Fisher had been a rich man, but he had given up that life to work for the poor. At his home that night were several people. But it was the words of two men that stayed with Jurgis. One man was Lucas, who used to be a preacher. Now he was a Socialist, traveling here and there to speak. The other man was Schliemann. He was a Swede.

Schliemann said he ate only what his body needed. Food cost him eleven cents a day. Every summer, during the harvest, he worked in the country. He would make one hundred and twenty-five dollars. That was enough for a year. A man could only live like this alone, he said. He would never marry. And no man should let himself fall in love until the Socialists took over.

Lucas talked about religion. He felt that once the Socialists took over, there would be a "New Jerusalem," and Heaven would be inside each one of us.

When Schliemann thought of that great day, he saw a perfect world—with no government at all. Everyone would do what he was interested in doing. If a person wanted to paint, he would find someone who was interested in looking at paintings. This person would help pay his way. The painter would work part of the time, too.

Of course, there was always work, like washing dishes, that no one wanted to do. Discoveries in science would take care of this kind of work. People would make machines that could wash and dry dishes.

Schliemann saw an end to cruel competition. Instead of competition, the cost of things would be decided this way: a thing would cost only what it took to make and deliver it.